In the Master's Hands

W. Phillip Keller

VINE
BOOKS

SERVANT BOOKS
Ann Arbor, Michigan

Published by Servant Books
P.O. Box 8617
Ann Arbor, Michigan 48107

Cover design by Michael Andaloro

This story is told in shortened form in Phillip Keller, *A Layman Looks at the Lord's Prayer.* Copyright 1976. Moody Press. Moody Bible Institute of Chicago.

Vine Books is an imprint of Servant Publications especially designed to serve Evangelical Christians.

Printed in the United States of America
ISBN 0-89283-330-0

87 88 89 90 91 10 9 8 7 6 5 4 3 2 1

Introduction

These lines are being penned high on the summit of The Great Divide in the northern Canadian Rockies. This is grand, still, awe-inspiring terrain, especially in autumn when mist and clouds drape the peaks in veils of mist. Frost has tinted the foliage with its first fall colors, and the frenzied, frantic sounds of modern man are far removed.

This is a spot to think long thoughts; to meditate quietly on the meaning of life; to search one's soul for simple yet profound realities which transcend time and our few fleeting years upon the planet.

The more so because for the past fourteen months my own life has been closely intertwined with fourteen families, each of whom faced terminal illness. Death has camped on their doorsteps. And at such times a man must ask some hard questions of his own hard heart.

Why am I here on earth?
What am I here for?
How shall I live?
What is the end?
Am I ready?

For the earnest, spiritual person who seeks eternal verities, the answers lie in his own relationship to God, our Father. He far transcends us mortals, so it follows that it is his desires for us, his earth children, which comprise the greatest good for man.

He it was who created us in his own wondrous love and generosity in order to share his own abundant, enduring life. It is his intention that we not only reciprocate his love, but in so doing we be conformed to his own character. Out of all this, his ultimate purpose is that we be fashioned according to his will so that in turn we should bring him enormous pleasure and profound satisfaction as we love and serve him with selfless abandonment.

Few, few Christians, who claim the name of Christ, clearly understand the noble, lofty objectives God has for them. They seldom know what it really means to be completely submissive to God's will, no matter the cost. They actually resist his purposes.

The hours I spent with a humble potter, high in the foothills of the Hindu Kush Mountains of Pakistan, taught me these truths in an unforgettable encounter. Though it was half a world away from here, it was an interlude of eternal worth to reveal truth.

What God by his gracious Spirit taught me that day has since been shared with thousands of others in lectures, in books, and on tapes. But once more it has been requested that the parable of the potter and the clay be retold in this little book.

My most earnest prayer is that the word pictures drawn here will be clear and sharp and enduring to benefit all who read. Possibly they will make as great an impact on those who pick up this book as they did on me at a time in my life when I longed to know Christ in intimate reality.

This incident took place about twenty-five years ago. Yet, so deeply were the truths of God's word etched on my spirit and inscribed on my tough will that they have not diminished in clarity. It was as if they had been drawn with the stiletto of a divine diamond, held firmly in the great yet gentle hand of my Father.

Only he knew how urgently I needed to understand his ways with me. In this simple yet profound parable, he taught me his own eternal truths about his will for me!

W. Phillip Keller
1986

IN THE MASTER'S HANDS

A writing and photographic assignment had taken me to visit various missionaries scattered in remote areas across the globe. One of these was a courageous young man working among the rugged Pathan people of northwest Pakistan.

This was Rudyard Kipling country, made famous by his dashing accounts of the Khyber Pass that stood on the frontier with Afghanistan. My visit there was in late November. Early snow already blanketed the gaunt, bare ridges of the Hindu Kush ranges. The local Pathans with whom we mingled roamed their grim valleys fully armed, rifles slung over their shoulders, bandoliers of bullets draped about their bodies.

We had gone into remote villages where my companion's fluent use of the local language and quiet affection for the people gave him ready entrance. We shared simple meals of roast lamb and boiled rice, delicious and nourishing in the biting cold. We chatted and laughed and told each other stories about managing sheep in the far places of the earth. The local tribesmen loved it, and quickly bonds of affection and mutual trust were forged between us.

One evening my companion, on an impulse no doubt stimulated by the gracious Spirit of God, asked me if I would care to visit a local china craftsman in the city of Peshawar. He had been to the potter's shop on various occasions to purchase fine pieces of his lovely wares. Perhaps it would be a special treat for me to see how beautiful vases, goblets, and bowls of exquisite design were made in the ancient traditions of the trade.

The suggestion excited me. Handcrafts have always fascinated me. Wood carving, weaving, stone cutting, shaping of brass or silver as done by primitive people all over the planet have always aroused my keenest interest. Watching a potter at work would be wonderful.

The next morning we walked quietly down a dusty back street into the busy bazaar of Peshawar. The long, low rays of the winter sun spread a mantle of golden warmth over the mountains. It was the morning light of a new day breaking over the rugged ranges rising behind the city. It was, unknown to me then, also the dawn of a new day of divine spiritual illumination that would sweep over my hard heart and stubborn spirit.

For at that point in my spiritual pilgrimage, my life, my aims, my ambitions were very much my own. I claimed to be a Christian, a follower of Christ. I insisted that my loyalty and love belonged to God my Father. Yet in fact I was still very much a strong-willed man who carved out his own career and decided the direction in which to move. Like most Christians I was one in name only.

My will had never yet been brought into harmony with that of the Most High.

My friend and I now jostled our way through ever-increasing crowds of local tribesmen who had come to buy or sell. We shared the narrow streets with camels, donkeys, and crude carts loaded with all sorts of wares and garden produce.

Finally we came to a crude little shop where a few pieces of lovely pottery stood in display on dusty shelves. An aged potter with stooped shoulders and a deeply furrowed face moved softly in the dark shadows of his establishment.

He did not see us at once. But the sound of my friend's voice attracted his attention. His features broke into a winsome smile when he recognized his visitor. With a wide sweep of his long thin arm, he invited us to enter his shop.

The usual formalities of a polite Eastern greeting were exchanged. I was introduced with gentle dignity as one who had come from afar. Cordial pleasantries were indulged as the old gentleman showed us some of his magnificent masterpieces.

Some of the pitchers, goblets, and bowls were the most exquisite handcrafted china I had ever held in my hands. The old gentleman explained with great patience that as a small lad he had been sent to the border country of China to learn the trade. There he worked for years as an apprentice to some of the most skilled artisans.

Noticing my genuine, sincere interest in his story and in his art, for it was just that, his eyes, tired and dim with long years in the dimness of his dark shop, began to glow with fresh fervor. "Would you care to watch me work on my wheel?" he murmured softly, almost as though he was apologizing for even suggesting the idea.

"Oh, yes!" I replied eagerly. "More, much more than that. Please show me every step you take from beginning to end in fashioning something lovely from a lump of crude clay!"

His response was immediate and positive. New vigor flowed through his frame. He had an audience! He would do a masterpiece.

Out of the comparable dimness of my own memory there began to come to me those simple, startling phrases from Jeremiah 18:2: "Arise, and go down to the potter's house, and there I will let you hear my words."

Little did I dream how clear, how dramatic, how profoundly God would speak to me that day in that dimly lit shop. He would convey to me as a man a message more emphatic than anything I had ever heard from any preacher in any pulpit.

The old potter crooked his bony fingers, and in that gesture so typical of the East, beckoned me to follow him to the back of his shop. It was so dark I almost had to feel my way through the gloom.

He swung open the rickety door to a small sheet metal shed that stood in the corner. A vile, repulsive, overpowering stench of decay engulfed my senses. I recoiled from the edge of the dark, black pit in the floor before me.

"What is this?" the unspoken

question swept through my subconscious. As if in reply, his simple statement startled me: "This is where the work begins!"

Wrapping his threadbare old cloak around him, the potter kneeled down beside the dark nauseating hole. Extending his long, lean arms into the pit, his skilled hands searched amid the lumpy clay for a fragment of earth exactly suited to his wishes. He took great pains to choose a clod of mud that would serve his needs.

Stooped over the pit, he paused to explain that a certain variety of local grass was added to the moist earth in the shed. The two were tramped together by his bony feet. The organic content of the plant fibers decaying in the mud added to the colloidal qualities of the clay. This accounted for the awful odors. But it also made for the finest earthenware.

Searching carefully, his skilled

and sensitive hands finally found the precise piece of clay he desired. He lifted it tenderly from the dark mass, molding it gently between his palms as he stood to his feet.

With a shattering impact the remarkable statements from Psalm 40 came crashing into my remembrance. In a flash of brilliant, lucid illumination I saw vividly what the inspired psalmist meant so long ago when he wrote: "I waited patiently for the Lord; and he inclined unto me, and heard my cry. He brought me up also out of an horrible pit, out of the miry clay" (Ps 40: 1, 2).

Yes, I too had been in the darkness of despair and degeneration and death. I had been in the place where there seemed to be no hope. I had been in the pit of degradation.

But the Master reached down one day and with loving care and tender skill picked me out, chose me, lifted me from my awful place. He had a special intention for me. Out of a lump of crude clay he would fashion something special. He and he alone would bring some beauty out of such earthy material.

Though I had watched the potter for only a few minutes, one salient aspect of his behavior impressed me more than anything else. Quite obviously he already had in mind the production of a magnificent masterpiece. He was not a casual craftsman. He was a true master of art.

Every movement he made, every step he took, every decision he carried out was done with the utmost care and precision. He was determined to make something of beauty and unique loveliness.

Gently he closed the door to the pit behind him. It creaked on its rusty hinges as if to say, "That's all for today!"

The stooped old gentleman slowly

shuffled across the shop. As he moved through the shadows he kept molding the lump of clay in his strong, sensitive hands. He pressed it and patted it until he had shaped it into a round, smooth ball of earth exactly the size best suited to his needs.

Did I wonder why at times I felt the hand of God shaping me? Did I recoil from the pressures often applied to my life, compressing my character, shaping my soul? Oh, yes, indeed God's Spirit was already speaking to my dull spirit very emphatically in that little shop.

In the center of his work area stood a massive round slab of stone. It was crudely cut and roughly chiseled from the rough rock of the mountains nearby. He told me he had used it all the years he worked in Peshawar.

With the greatest care he placed the ball of clay exactly in the center of the stone. It really astonished me what pains he took to place it precisely where he could handle it best. Then drawing up a well-worn stool he sat down before the stone.

I noticed that he had a very primitive, treadlelike piece of equipment which he operated with his feet. This arrangement made him able to start or stop turning the wheel. He could whirl the rock very rapidly or he could rotate it very slowly, whichever he chose.

Strangely, emphatically, clearly the Word of the Lord came to me again from Psalm 40:2: he "set my feet upon a rock, and established my goings."

It was the Master who had in truth lifted me out of the awful pit of my old, disgusting life. It was he who would center me in Christ. It was his compassion which by his grace could set me going in a new direction.

Never before had I fully seen or understood all of this. I could not comprehend clearly how I was but a bit of earth in which God's will was being worked out. No wonder Jesus taught us to pray humbly: "Thy will be done on earth as it is in heaven." Yes, in this chunk of clay, this clod of mud, this bit of earth between his strong hands. Yes, in my little life.

Out of sheer necessity, for there is no other way, I had to be centered and grounded upon the Rock of God—Christ.

Here I was, a fragment of clay, formless and as yet unfashioned, under the intimate touch of the Master's strong and knowing hands. What hope, what assurance, what wondrous consolation!

As I watched the potter begin to whirl the stone, I was galvanized by the intense look in his face. He could see more than a mere lump of clay turning on that stone. He could see emerging from the mud a vessel of lovely perfection and exquisite design. It was his desire above all else to turn out a goblet that would gleam with rare beauty and unusual grace.

He told us so. He said that was what he had in mind. That was his intention. That was his will. There was in this crude clay an enormous potential for a vessel to emerge for noble and lofty service. His highest hopes and keenest aspirations were that an article of rare art and great use should come from the clay.

It dawned on my hard heart just then, that is exactly what my Father has in mind for me!

Like so many people I had often felt that the intentions of God toward me were harsh and severe. Not until this day did I comprehend clearly the generous and noble hope he held for my well-being. His honor was at stake in me. From this life of mine he longed to produce a vessel of honor that could and would serve him well, doing noble service.

"But in a great house there are not only vessels of gold and of silver, but also of wood and of earth; and some to honor, and some to dishonor" (2 Tm 2:20).

Little wonder that a special intensity pervaded the lined features of the aged craftsman as he began to turn the great slab of stone with a small treadle operated by his bare and bony feet.

The gleam in his eyes told me he intended to so impress his will on the clay that it would become a handsome article of great worth. His expression was one which combined joy, hope and eager anticipation.

God's gracious, gentle Spirit spoke to me softly but surely in the dim light of that dusty shop, saying, "Can you sense the eager excitement which fills your Father's heart as he looks upon you in love and holds you in his great strong hands? How he yearns to accomplish his will in your life—in this bit of earth—so a bit of heaven can be produced in your life."

The impact of this insight was akin to having scales of unbelief removed from my spiritual eyes of understanding. As I watched the potter, I was entranced by the obvious tenderness and care with which he handled the artifact he was shaping with such skill.

Both in truth and in fact I was being taken back to Jeremiah 18:3: "Then I went down to the potter's house, and, behold, he wrought a work on the wheels."

Since I had never watched anyone work with clay before, it especially fascinated me to discover that it was done through the medium of water. Beside the little rickety stool on which he sat, the old man had placed two bowls of water, one on either side. Not once did he touch the mud, now spinning very swiftly at the center of the wheel, without first dipping his fingers in the fluid.

As he applied the art and skill of all his years to the piece, it was always through the medium of the moisture on his hands. Smoothly, deftly his delicate fingers and skilled palms pressed in upon the clay. It astounded me to see how readily the material responded to the master's touch. Before my eyes an elegant goblet of graceful proportions took shape beneath those knowing hands.

But always, always, the work went on through the use of water. Through the moisture the master craftsman's will and wishes were being transmitted in clay. His intentions were actually being carried out in this bit of earth in this simple yet unusual way.

Suddenly there burst upon my spirit a new awareness. This is exactly how God always deals with me!

Though he does, in fact, hold me in his own great hands, it is always, always through the wondrous water of his own Word that his will and wishes are transmitted to me. His own divine declaration impresses upon my hard heart and stony spirit what his intentions are for me. It is through his Word that he makes known to me his gracious desires in shaping my character to conform to his own.

For me as a man this was a crucial discovery. I understood now how important it was to come under the influence of the Scriptures—to respond in confidence and faith to their impact—to quietly comply with the commands of Christ with hearty obedience and generous goodwill.

As if to emphasize this point the stone suddenly stopped. Why? I looked on in astonishment. I bent over to see what had happened. Why was the work at a standstill?

The potter picked up a fine straw from the bench beside him. With the utmost care he removed a small grain of grit from the side of the goblet.

His skilled fingers had felt the sudden resistance of the grain of sand to his touch. Once again he began to turn the stone. The wheel now whirled with increased velocity. With great expertise he smoothed the shining surface of the goblet again. All would be well.

But it was not to be! Just as suddenly the stone stopped a second time. Once more with astonishing care he pried another hard object—another tiny grain of sand—from the side of the goblet. It had gouged an ugly scar in the lovely vessel, visible even to my untrained vision.

A strained look of both anxiety and concern began to steal over the potter's face. A sense of foreboding began to cloud his eyes. Did the clay carry within it other fragments of sand or grit or gravel? Would these resistant elements thwart his will and wreck his work? Would all of his finest intentions, his highest hopes, his wonderful wishes come to nothing?

It depended on the content of the clay. Time would tell.

Once more the stone began to turn. But just as suddenly it stopped a third time. The potter's shoulders slumped disconsolately. An abject look of dismay welled up in his tired eyes. In despair he pointed to a deep, ragged gouge that cut an angry gash in the body of the beautiful goblet. It was ruined beyond repair.

In a gesture of frustration and utter futility he crushed the clay down upon the wheel. Beneath his hands it was again a formless mass of mud lying in a dark heap upon the stone.

"And the vessel that he made of clay was marred in the hand of the potter" (Jer 18:4).

Oh the titanic truth of that

ancient statement in Scripture. How often in thousands upon thousands of lives the superb work of the Master had been marred beyond remedy. The lesson came home to me with the explosive power of the dynamic truth released in me by God's own Spirit.

Why was this rare and lovely masterpiece ruined in the master's hands?

Because he had run into resistance. The truth burst about me like a crash of thunder and flash of lightning.

Was this happening in my life? Were God's finest intentions for me being frustrated by the hardness of my heart, the tough intransigence of my will? Was the patience of my Master in trying to perfect me coming to nothing?

I was a man well into the middle of life. The first forty years were already past and gone with not much of eternal worth to show for them. Was my character to be marred and made of no account? Would I end up a grief to God, a total disaster under the gracious hands of the divine Potter?

Obviously the choices were mine as to what would happen. Either I could decide to comply with Christ's commands—to comply with my Father's wishes and submit to the gracious sovereignty of his Spirit— or I could prefer to go my own way, exercise my own will, and stubbornly execute my own wishes in opposition to God.

In dismay and pity I turned to my friend and asked him in a low whisper, "What will the potter do now?" The urgent question was passed on. For a few moments it seemed to hang suspended, unanswered like a dark cloud in the oppressive atmosphere of that dingy shop.

Then the potter turned to look at me from his wobbly stool. His eyes were clouded, sad, like deep wells filled with remorse. He spoke softly, hesitantly. "I will just make a crude peasant's finger bowl from the same clay!" His tired frame seemed more bent than ever. What a burden this was for him to bear!

Smoothly the rugged rock began to whirl again. A subdued, heavy stillness pervaded the place. None of us spoke. Swiftly, deftly, with a minimum of time, a very plain little finger bowl was shaped on the wheel. What might have been a rare and gorgeous goblet was now no more than a common little vessel to be used in some peasant's crude hovel.

The master craftsman was obliged to set aside his first and finest intentions. What had come from his hands now was second best. A bit of earth, a piece of clay that might have graced a king's palace or some royal residence, was now destined for menial service of little worth.

So it was that the Word of God

came to me with penetrating power: ". . . so he [God] made it again another vessel, as seemed good to the potter to make it" (Jer 18:4).

In the lowly, humble surroundings of that potter's shed in Peshawar I had to ask myself some searching, sobering questions! They would begin to alter the whole direction of my life from that day onwards. Here they are:

Am I going to be a piece of fine china or just a common finger bowl?

Is my life going to be a noble goblet fit to contain the fine wine of Christ's very life from which others can drink and be refreshed?

Or am I to be only a clay finger bowl in which others dabble their fingers merely to pass on and forget all about it?

It was one of the most solemn and serious moments in the whole of my spiritual pilgrimage. Very rarely had I been so acutely aware that my Father was speaking to me very intimately, very directly, by the events around me.

"Father, thy will be done in earth, (in clay), in this human clay of my life, as it is done in heaven."

Do I really mean this? Do I really want it? Do I really intend to have it happen to me?

These are penetrating questions which every Christian, at some point in life, simply must face. Are we going to do God's will or are we not? Will we submit to his wishes and comply with his commands or not?

When Jesus Christ was here among us, he constantly reiterated that he was here to do the Father's will. His entire life of such impeccable conduct was a living demonstration that he did only the will of his Father. This utter compliance with the wondrous will of God was the means whereby he secured our salvation and brought us from death to life.

It follows, then, that if we are to be his people, he calls us to submit ourselves to his blessed wishes. And as we live in harmony with him, our lives, too, can become fit vessels of great honor to his name.

Though the Pakistani potter was not fully satisfied with the rather ordinary outcome of his labor, he was still intent on completing the process of making the piece so I could see how it was done. I had several more stern lessons to learn in that simple shop.

Quietly he reached up and lifted a very fine thread, almost as slender as a human hair, from where it hung above his wheel. With meticulous care he dipped the thread in the water bowl at his right side until it was thoroughly soaked in the liquid.

Then he put the wheel in motion again. The little finger bowl so

freshly formed from the pliant clay
whirled softly at the center of the
great stone. It was perfectly round,
perfectly shaped.

Taking the wet thread in his two
strong, slender hands, he pulled it
taut between them. Then with a
swift, sure motion drew it smoothly
across the base of the little bowl.
The smooth action deftly separated
the fresh piece from the lump of
mud from which it had been
shaped.

This done, he stopped the stone.
A long, low sigh escaped his lips. A
sad, faraway look filled his tired
eyes. It seemed his rounded
shoulders slumped deeper than
ever.

"It is only a finger bowl!" he
mused, speaking as much to himself
as to me. "But it takes as much care
as if it was indeed a gorgeous
goblet."

During the pause that followed,
the Spirit of God spoke again in

profound clarity. "There comes the time when the one fashioned under the Master's hand simply must be cut off, separated from the old ways, the old life, the former habits, the previous attitudes. There is a detachment necessary for the newly formed vessel to be set aside for special service."

This principle is one which many so-called Christians have difficulty grasping. I was one of them at that point in my life. The process of being set apart from my contemporaries and the milieu of the world system from which I was chosen by God appeared to be rather too severe.

Jesus' startling statement came home to my heart with tremendous impact as I watched the potter stand to his feet and lift the tiny vessel tenderly between his hands. "Ye have not chosen me, but I have chosen you, and ordained you. . . ." What for? "That ye should go and bring forth fruit, and that your fruit should remain" (Jn 15:16).

With the utmost care the aged craftsman glided across the little shed and set the raw, green piece on a shelf nailed to the wall. In a low voice he whispered to us, "It must sit there quite a long while until the clay cures properly." Then as an afterthought he added, "You see, this kind of work is not done in a day. It takes time, lots and lots of time, to turn out fine china."

Most of my early life I had always been such an impetuous person. I was so impatient to get on with things. My driving disposition often demanded instant action and immediate results.

But God my Father was not like that. He never seemed rushed and hurried to achieve his ends. He took so much time and care and loving patience to perfect his work on the planet. Whether it was growing a mighty oak, shaping a majestic mountain, or fashioning a human character, it all took time, time, time. His work was not done in a day!

It dawned on my dull spirit that morning as I stood gazing at the array of chinaware on the potter's shelves that it would take months, years, a lifetime for me to be brought to full maturity in the Master's tender hands. There would be long spells in life when I, too, would feel very much that I was simply "set on the shelf."

These would not be easy interludes for a man with my personality. One of the most difficult lessons for me to ever learn was to wait for God to move. To wait for him to pick me up and take me on to the next stage of maturity. To wait for him to perfect his purposes in me.

We of the western world are so keen to be on the go—for God. We attach so much importance to being

in the whirl of things. We demand
action, action, action at all times!

Our ways are not necessarily the
Master's ways. Nor are our human
impulses his desires. And we do well
to realize that there will be times
when he sees fit to set us aside in
stillness and quietness to achieve
his finest intentions for us. The
painful waiting is one of the means
used for our ultimate improvement.
In humble acceptance of his
arrangements, there lies peace.

"Be still, and know that I am God:
I will be exalted among the heathen,
I will be exalted in the earth!" (Ps
46:10). Yes, in this bit of human
clay, in this fragment of the earth,
God will be honored in me.

Those special moments in the
hushed atmosphere of that dusty
spot were to change my entire
perspective on life for the rest of my
days. For the first time I saw clearly
God my Father's view of his divine
work in the world. He was bringing

sons and daughters to glory by conforming them to his own wondrous character.

This is why he made me. This is why I was here. This is what he intended for me as his new creation, the special one in his care.

But the potter was not yet done with demonstrating all of his skill to us. He crooked a bony finger in my direction, giving me the ancient sign to follow him to his tiny furnace room. It could hardly be called that. It would be better described as a corner of his crude establishment where the final glaze was put on his pottery.

I had often wondered just how this was done. I love beautiful handcrafted pieces, no matter whether they be paintings, carvings, pottery, or even handwoven pieces.

Earlier that morning I had gazed in wonderment and awe at the gorgeous goblets, vases, pitchers, and plates which adorned this

master craftsman's display cases.
They were some of the most
exquisite china I had ever seen
anywhere in the world, and I had
traveled in some thirty countries.

There was a patina of perfection
on his pieces that I had seldom seen
before. They literally glowed with a
rare and remarkable beauty. They
were in truth masterpieces.

The old gentleman invited me to
stoop down and peer through a
small quartz window into the fierce
fires of his retort. Just the heat
radiating from it made me draw
back lest I be burned.

"This is where the final glaze is
put on the pottery." A strange little
smile played about his lips. "Most
people do not know that fine china
comes from fierce fires." He looked
away softly into the dark shadows
of his shop. "You cannot get beauty
without some severe suffering!"

It was a profound philosophical
statement. It was more than that; it

was a powerful spiritual principle. Perhaps he spoke it with such deep conviction because it reflected the sum total of his own hard life in this dingy place.

Year after year, season after season, there had come from this dusty little shop on a side street in Peshawar some of the most lovely china in the world. Out of the furnace of his own affliction there had emerged exquisite pieces of wondrous beauty to enrich many homes and serve many lives.

As if to put the final touch on all that he had shown me that morning, the potter looked me full in the face, his eyes now bright with intensity. "You see, my name, my reputation, my honor are at stake in my work!"

In a sudden flash of vivid illumination this precise parallel came home to my spirit. God's name, his reputation, his honor were likewise at stake in me. Did my character and conduct reflect his life?

I could see now why it was that at times he would have to put me, too, into "the furnace of affliction," as we call it in our contemporary culture. Actually such experiences are not something we can shrug off with a smile. They sear our souls and subject our spirits to enormous suffering. Often they carry fierce physical pain as well.

Little did I realize that day what great suffering lay ahead for me. There would be times of such stern testing, such burning heartache, such severe sorrow that the trivia and tinsel of life would be consumed in the refining.

I began to find in life that the most remarkable people, the most lovely characters, the most shining souls were those who had in truth been "through the fire." These were the ones with that special quality in their lives that drew me to them with awe, wonder, respect, and love.

They were masterpieces who had submitted to the severe but noble purposes of God. They had accepted and approved of his ways.

Of course, we see this demonstrated most dramatically in the life and death of our Lord Jesus Christ. To submit himself to his Father's will cost him shame, suffering, and ignominy beyond our human comprehension. But because of it there emerged from his earth experience a splendor and a salvation that has touched millions upon millions of lives all across human history.

Out of our death he brings life.

Out of our darkness he brings light.

Out of our despair he brings love.

It is this glorious enterprise in which he is engaged in the earth. He invites us as his people to share in his sufferings. He has been here, he has lived where we live, he has endured our sorrows as we do. He understands us fully.

It is he, the Master Craftsman, who is creating in us his own sublime workmanship. He is perfecting beautiful people. He is setting us apart for special service to all his earth children.

His name, his honor, his reputation are at stake in us. To him be the glory, forever!

Other Books of Interest from Servant Books

God in Our Midst
James I. Packer

J.I. Packer believes that God's people urgently need revival. He tells us what renewal is and then explains how to get there. *$1.95*

True Confessions
Owning Up to the Secret Everybody Knows
Philip Yancey

In *True Confessions* Philip Yancey asks the question, "Whatever became of sin?" With personal examples, he points out that life with God involves taking responsibility for our wrongdoing and trusting in the love of God for forgiveness. *$1.95*

To Live or Die
Facing Decisions at the End of Life
C. Everett Koop, M.D.

Dr. Koop explores the complex issues surrounding death and dying and offers a Christian approach to making decisions, for oneself and others. *$1.95*

Women: the Challenge and the Call
Dee Jepsen

It is time for both men and women to understand the vital importance of a woman's contributions in the church and in society. Dee Jepsen calls women to assert themselves against the forces that threaten to destroy family life—widespread pornography, the erosion of respect for human life, and the pursuit of selfishness. *$1.95*

Available at your Christian bookstore or from
**Servant Publications • Dept. 209 • P.O. Box 7455
Ann Arbor, Michigan 48107**
Please include payment plus $.75 per book
for postage and handling
*Send for your FREE catalog of Christian
books, music, and cassettes.*